Miniature Horses

by Alix Wood

WINDMILL BOOKS

New York

Published in 2017 by **Windmill Books**, An Imprint of Rosen Publishing
29 East 21st Street, New York, NY 10010

Editor: Eloise Macgregor
Designer: Alix Wood

Photo Credits: Cover, 1, 11 © Dollar Photo Club; 3, 4, 12-13, 19 bottom right, 21 top, 22, 27 © Adobe Stock; 6 bottom, 7, 9, 29 © Shutterstock; 8 G Caspian Horse Society; 10 © Duncan C; 14 © Beamish Museum Ltd; 15 © James Tworow; 16 © Grand Oak Photos; 17 © Gkuchera/Dreamstime; 18 © Loshadenok /Dreamstime; 19 top and middle © Harry Thompson; 20 © Dreamstime; 21 bottom © Beyond DC; 23 © Barbara Mielewczyk/ Tierfotoagentur/FLPA; 25 © Erik S. Lesser; 26 © ClatieK; 28 © Sarah D

Cataloging-in-Publication Data
Names: Wood, Alix.
Title: Miniature horses / Alix Wood.
Description: New York : Windmill Books, 2017. | Series: Mini animals| Includes index.
Identifiers: ISBN 9781499481617 (pbk.) | ISBN 9781499481624 (library bound) |
  ISBN 9781508192985 (6 pack)
Subjects: LCSH: Miniature horses--Juvenile literature.
Classification: LCC SF293.M56 W66 2017 | DDC 636.1'09--dc23

Manufactured in the United States of America
CPSIA Compliance Information: Batch #: BW17PK. For Further Information contact: Windmill Books, New York, New York at 1-866-478-0556

Contents

Adorable Mini Horses

Imagine a full-grown horse that is around the size of a large dog! Miniature horses are not the same as ponies. They are much shorter than even the smallest breed of pony.

Ponies are usually **stocky**, with short legs and necks. Most mini horse **breeders** prefer their animals to have longer legs and necks, like the mini horse in the picture below. Some mini horses like these pictured right look more like ponies.

Miniature horses can come in all sorts of colors. This chestnut-colored mare has had a **pinto** foal. A pinto horse has patches of white and another color.

Cute Alert!

This foal is only 20 inches (50 cm) tall! That is around the same height as a Labrador Retriever dog.

A Horse or a Pony?

Probably the most well-known small horse breeds are the Falabella and the Shetland pony. The Shetland is called a pony, but the smaller Falabella is called a horse. Why?

It's not because of their height. Usually, if a horse is under 14.2 hands it is a pony. If it is over 14.2 hands it is a horse. Shetland ponies are usually less than 11 hands high. Falabellas are usually less than 8 hands high!

Horses are measured in hands. A hand is 4 inches (10 cm) wide. Is yours?

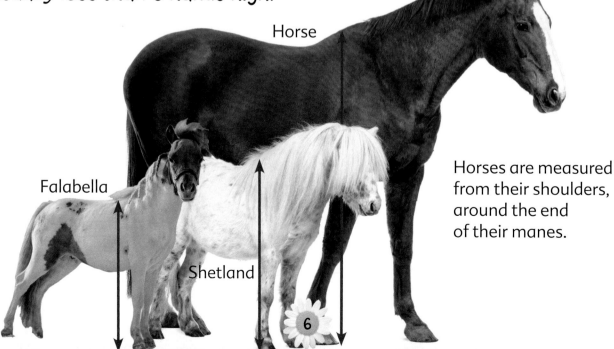

Horse

Falabella

Shetland

Horses are measured from their shoulders, around the end of their manes.

6

Any fully-grown horse or pony less than 34 inches (86.4 cm) tall is classified as a miniature horse. There are several different breeds of miniature horse. This foal is a Falabella.

Why Are Minis So Small?

In most cases, mini horses have been created by horse lovers using **selective breeding**. Horse breeders choose their smallest horses to have foals. They then select the smallest of these foals to have more foals. Over time, each **generation** of horses gets smaller and smaller.

There are many different reasons why people want tiny horses. Miniature horses were bred in Europe in the 1600s as fashionable pets for the rich. French king Louis XIV kept mini horses at his palace at Versailles around 1650.

Tough little miniature pony breeds were created to work in coal mines. Their small size helped them work in the cramped conditions.

These tiny Caspian horses come from Iran.

Falabella horses, like this foal, come from South America. Horses brought to the region by Spanish settlers found little grass to eat. Because of this, over generations the horses got smaller.

Shetland Ponies

Shetland ponies come from the Shetland Isles, a group of islands off the coast of Scotland. The hills and moors where the ponies live can be very cold and windy. Not all Shetland ponies are classified as miniature horses. Many are too tall.

Shetland Isles

Shetland ponies have very thick coats of fur. They grow a double coat in winter with special outer hairs to help shed the rain. Their thick winter coats and thick manes and tails help protect the ponies.

Shetland ponies are the strongest of all horse and pony breeds. They can pull twice their own weight. Heavy draft horses can only pull about half their own weight!

Falabellas

Looking like tiny versions of their **Thoroughbred** horse relatives, Falabellas are one of the smallest miniature horse breeds. They are very intelligent and easily trained.

Because of their intelligence Falabellas can easily be taught how to pull carts, jump over obstacles, and even work as guide animals.

Cute Alert!

Falabellas are too small to be ridden by anyone except a very small child.

These Falabella foals have the long legs and body shape of a horse, not the short legs and stocky body of a pony. That is why they are classified as horses.

Working Ponies

Many of the earliest miniature horses in Europe were bred to work in cramped coal mines. Known as "pit ponies," these small, strong horses could pull heavy carts along the narrow tunnels. Horses working in deep coal mines were lowered down using a **hoist**. Once in the pit, they were stabled underground, and never saw daylight.

In the late 1800s it is believed there were more than 200,000 horses at work in British mines!

The coal mines of West Virginia, Virginia, and Kentucky were very small. Ponies had to be smaller than 34 inches (86.4 cm) high to work there. Although life was hard for the pit ponies, they developed a strong bond with their handlers. It is said that if the lights failed, a pony would stop until its handler had hold of its tail. Then the pony would lead them to safety!

Miniature horses can be trained to pull carts. Their low height makes the horses very stable. This helps them pull surprisingly large weights.

Cute Alert!

Some owners make tiny stagecoaches or covered wagons like the one above for their mini horses to pull.

Miniature Foals

Like other horse breeds, miniature **mares** usually give birth in the spring. They will have carried their foals for eleven months. The foal stays with its mother for the first few months.

A newborn mini horse weighs about the same as a small beagle dog. A foal can stand on its own feet within minutes of being born! In just a few hours the foal is able to run and jump.

Horses are **mammals**. Their young drink milk produced by the mother. The foal below is nuzzling its mother, looking for milk.

Cute Alert!

This foal is only one day old. It is getting used to wearing its tiny **head collar**. Mini foals are usually very friendly, like this one.

17

Caring for a Mini Horse

A miniature horse need less room to **graze** and less food to eat than a full-sized horse. However, it still needs the same amount of care, such as regular grooming, and veterinary and dental care.

mane

forelock

Cute Alert!

We can all have bad hair days, even mini horses! Manes and forelocks can go a little wild. Regular grooming should help.

Miniature horses need to have their teeth checked regularly. Uneven wear causes sharp edges that can make it painful for the horse to eat.

How to Groom a Mini Horse

Grooming keeps a horse's coat healthy and helps build a friendship between the mini horse and its owner.

1 Brush the face with a soft bristle body brush.

body brush

2 Gently brush the forelock, mane, and tail using a pin-cushion brush. Start from the bottom of the tail and work your way up.

pin-cushion brush

3 Using circular motions brush the body with a rubber curry. Clean away the loose dust and hair using a body brush.

rubber curry

4 Carefully pick out any stones and dirt stuck in the hoof using a hoof pick. Clean from heel to toe, to avoid jabbing the delicate frog area of the hoof.

frog

hoof pick

Food, Fields, and Shelter

Because of their small size, you can keep a miniature horse in a big backyard! One acre of **pasture** would feed around two to three mini horses. They need some shelter to escape from bad weather. Miniature horses also need plenty of clean, fresh water to drink.

It is important that a miniature horse has space to run around and get some exercise, too.

The bottom of a stable can get quite musty. Because miniature horses are low to the ground, it is important to keep their stable clean. It's also necessary to make sure their stables get a good flow of fresh air.

Cute Alert!

These owners have cut a window in the stable door to help airflow and so their mini horse can see out!

21

Mini Horses as Pets

Miniature horses make great pets. They suit people who love horses but don't have room for a full-sized version. Other people keep them for their very young children to ride. Children up to around 60 pounds (27 kg) can ride a mini horse. Their friendly nature means they make great company.

Mini horses are probably so friendly because they are usually picked up and cuddled from an early age. It's hard to resist picking up a fluffy mini foal and petting it.

Keeping miniature horses is becoming more and more popular. You may be able to see some at your local county fair.

Mini Horses That Help

One advantage of being small is that miniature horses can go places most horses can't go. Some organizations use mini **therapy** horses to visit patients in hospitals or to visit retirement homes. The cute horses help cheer people up. Walking a horse can inspire patients to exercise more than they might have done, too.

Therapy horses are trained to get used to the sights and sounds of a hospital before they can start work.

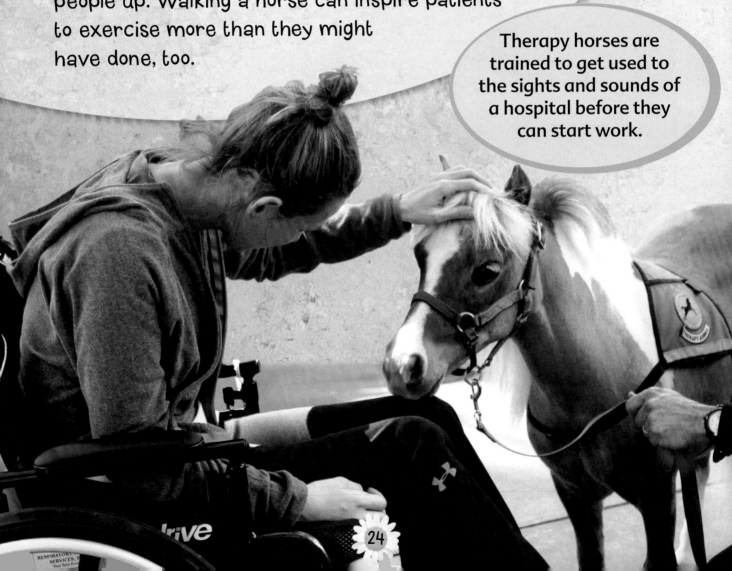

24

Miniature horses can be used to guide people with poor eyesight. Some people prefer a guide horse to a guide dog. People can be allergic to or frightened of dogs. Also, horses live longer than dogs which means the partnership between a horse and their owner can last longer.

Owners need to have a suitable space outdoors for when their guide horse is "off-duty." They need more toilet breaks than dogs do, too!

Cute Alert!

Guide horses wear sneakers! The shoes keep the horses from slipping on shiny floors and protects them from hot surfaces and sharp objects.

At the Showground

Horse shows can be fun events. People who own miniature horses can enter them in competitions. There are often classes for children to enter, such as youth showmanship classes. Contestants must be neatly dressed, and have groomed their horses themselves.

Cute Alert!

Before a show, owners often give their horse a **pedicure**! They wash, clean, and even paint their horse's hooves.

Mini horses can enter classes which judge their looks, or how they pull a cart, or how they jump over obstacles. Full-sized horses are ridden in jumping classes. As minis are too small to ride, the handler runs alongside the horse instead.

When a horse wins a class they usually get a ribbon to pin on their head collar. Different countries have different color ribbons for 1st, 2nd, and 3rd.

	USA	Canada	Britain
1st	Blue	Red	Red
2nd	Red	Blue	Blue
3rd	Yellow	White	Yellow

Some horse shows have obstacle course classes. The horse and their handler must go over, under, and through various obstacles.

Test Your Knowledge

1. Which of these units are horses sometimes measured using?
   a) hands b) heads c) arms

2. Which measurement to its shoulder must a horse be less than to be known as a miniature horse?
   a) 12 inches (30.5 cm)
   b) 34 inches (86.4 cm)
   c) 60 inches (152.4 cm)

3. Is a Falabella
   a) a horse b) a pony?

4. How long do mares carry their foals before they give birth?
   a) two years
   b) 11 months
   c) five weeks

5 Why did Falabella horses become small?
   a) they had an illness
   b) they didn't get much sunlight
   c) they had little food to eat

6 What helps Shetland ponies
   keep warm?
   a) their thick coats of fur
   b) running around all day
   c) their short legs

7 What would you use a hoof pick for?
   a) choosing what color to paint
      a horse's hooves
   b) lifting up a horses legs
   c) picking stones out of a horse's hooves

8 Why do some blind people prefer
   a miniature guide horse to a guide dog?
   a) the people are allergic to dogs
   b) horses live longer than dogs
   c) both a and b

How did you do? The answers are on page 32.

Glossary

breeders People who raise animals to produce the animals' young.

generation A group of individuals born and living at the same time.

graze To feed on growing grass or herbs.

head collar A set of straps enclosing an animal's head to which a lead may be attached.

hoist A mechanism to raise and lower objects.

mammals Warm-blooded animals that have a backbone and hair, breathe air, and feed milk to their young.

mares Adult female horses.

pasture Land used for grazing.

pedicure Care of the feet, toes, and toenails.

pinto A horse or pony marked with patches of white and another color.

selective breeding The intentional breeding of animals to produce offspring with desired characteristics.

stocky Thickset.

therapy The treatment of disorders or injuries.

Thoroughbred A breed of horses, bred chiefly for racing, originating from crosses between Arabian stallions and English mares.

Further Information

Books

Linde, Barbara M. *Miniature Horses (Horsing Around)*. New York, NY: Gareth Stevens Publishing, 2011.

Matzke, Ann. *Mini Horse (You Have a Pet What?!)*. Vero Beach, FL: Rourke Educational Media, 2015.

Silverstein, Alvin. *Miniature Horses: Cool Pets! (Far-Out and Unusual Pets)*. Berkeley Heights, NJ: Enslow Elementary, 2012.

Websites

For web resources related to the subject of this book, go to: **www.windmillbooks.com/weblinks** and select this book's title.

Index

Answers 1) a, 2) b, 3) a, 4) b, 5) c, 6) a, 7) c, 8) c